I0170833

ZEN IN THE CITY

A COLLECTION OF POEMS TO GUIDE YOU HOME

MELISSA MONROE

ROOTED WHOLENESS PRESS

Published by:

ROOTED WHOLENESS PRESS
P.O. Box 3022
McKinney, Texas 75072
www.rootedwholeness.com

Cover design by:
Arash Jahani

ISBN: paperback 978-1-7331458-0-0
ISBN: eBook 978-1-7331458-1-7

Map Makers

If it wasn't for my Ayurveda teachers and the gurus and rishis before them, I may not have healed enough to remember I love poetry. It's hard to connect to beauty, and definitely the divine when you're chasing a life and version of you that's like wearing tight pants all day.

To my fellow roller coaster companion, Mark, thank you for reminding me how long and how deeply I've wanted to write. Thank you for strapping yourself in alongside me when we didn't know where we were headed on this healing transformation. We've experienced steep climbs and plummeting falls, jerky twists, and quick drops that made us laugh and scream, but we always walked away holding hands.

To my spirit guides and the marvelous, universal energy buzzing around us all, thank you for lighting the way.

Signed December 6, 2020 and Feb 9 2021

CONTENTS

Context   vii
Pilates class   xi

ONE   1
- *a prayer and a poem*   5
- *heart breath*   6
- *the heart pact*   7
- *splinters*   8
- *4:48*   9
- *tick tock*   10
- *city sunrise*   12
- *paper focus*   13
- *midday*   14
- *the thinking pipeline*   15
- *the whispers*   16
- *love note*   17

TWO   19
-*sky sublime*   21
- *bluejay breakfast*   23
- *becoming art*   24
- *becoming*   26
- *becoming waves*   28
- *choose*   29
- *scavenger hunt*   30
- *spaces*   31
- *whispering heart*   32
- *morning drive*   34
- *lioness*   36

THREE   38
- *Autumn, my muse.*   40
- *old trees*   42
- *country road*   43
- *cream cheese at night*   44

-my backyard at night..45
- surrender..47
- magnolia tree..48
- stethoscope...50
- the dinner party, 1..51
- thawed out...53
- hue..54
- lover's kiss...56

FOUR...57
- what senses are for...59
- the gardener's prayer..60
- tango...61
- take a drink..62
- prayer of moonbeams..64
- the messenger..65
- on meditation...66
- the vessel...68
- belonging to you...69
- interior song...71
- the walk...72

Extra chapters are like spice....................................75
A Word..79
Index...81
About the Author...87

CONTEXT

TRANSFORMATIVE YEARS

Who's lived through a transformative period in history? An unprecedented event? At some point, everyone will have a day that's newsworthy.

I started this book fall of 2018. I was a newbie writer (*again*), and the poems were completed by fall of 2019. Now it was time to write the preface. After reworking it several times, it finally flowed. It was February 2020, a few weeks before my oldest daughter's wedding, and a few weeks before COVID-19 hit the U.S. news cycle.

Something didn't feel right with "The Starbucks Chapter," so I shelved it. Luckily, I'd made a pact with myself that I'd only write when feeling ease. The chapter was about people in a bustling coffee shop. Shelving it turned out to be a good call.

With a background in biology and epidemiology, I initially expected the pandemic to last the year. By May, my estimates were closer to fall of 2021.

Many of us worried about jobs, money, our children, our grandchildren. We felt uncertainty around relationships, work, routines, and health. There was a constant stream of news about economic and personal tragedies. Businesses were closing doors, people were unable to pay rent, and there were increases in domestic violence, divorce, anxiety, mental health issues, and deaths.

The year of 2020 merged into 2021. The pandemic continued, and blended with social, cultural, and political unrest. It all rolled into a sort of global ball of yarn and paradigm shift in slow motion.

Prejudice based crimes and public rage prompted the names of George Floyd, Breonna Taylor, and Soon Chung Park to be household reminders. If we dared look, their stories unveiled systemic, long term violence, fear, loathing, and abuse of power.

Months of interrupted schedules blended with strife between ethnicities, cultures, economic statuses, personal views, vaccine preferences, and more. Intolerance soared. To my ears, this all seemed like a beckoning from nature, energy, history, and the divine to awaken and love. Just then, political unrest peaked.

I've never seen (*was there ever?*) a storming of the U.S. capital with participants claiming they were acting on behalf of the sitting president. But now that I've reminded you of all this, breathe.

Humans have lived through wars, violence, aggression, multiple types of slavery and numerous types of abuse. People have been acting out their wounds, insecurities, narcissism, and sociopathy for millennia.

Here's the point. This book is about love, compassion, and understanding. It's about Zen in the *midst* of all that is. Peace in the *midst* of all that has happened, can happen, and will happen. I'm not saying overlook it. I'm not saying don't act. I'm saying, let's hold space for love. Let's learn from history. Let's hold space for beauty. Because stress and animosity can't be the end of the story.

The ginkgo tree has lived through every war in modern

history, through every shortage both natural and human made, through every paradigm shift, and every tragedy since the age of dinosaurs. It continues to grow. We cannot let fear or hate consume or direct us. Love is waiting to sprout and persist.

This book is born out of great cultural and paradigm shifts, written as a woman, mother of three, and lover of life, who wants so much more for myself and others than I sometimes see. But there's a lot of beauty out there too. And even though it's more quiet—it whispers and waits for us to come visit *it*, but it occurs to me that both love and beauty might ripple farther and faster due to their lightness of being.

Love where you can.

Melissa

PILATES CLASS
WHY NEUTRAL IS A GOOD THING

In 1986, I taught my first aerobics class. By 1988, I was knee deep in leg warmers, big hair, loud music, and shiny leotards. My job was to command the room—to lead people to do what I wanted them to do and how and when I wanted them to do it.

The drill was to use popular music blaring through surround speakers while shouting basic directions over the noise. "Four knees up, now walk it back." "Two to the right. Two to the left." This was paired with skyrocketing my body around the room like a sort of a moving billboard.

Thankfully, some gyms and classes have since softened their approach. A few places understand and allow for people to get their heart rate up while providing a more pleasant, beautiful, and balancing environment. I'm glad because the orange, purple, and red walls as a backdrop for dirty, metal chairs and bacteria-ridden hanging mats just isn't cutting it.

Pilates taught me to respect others more deeply. To understand that everyone's body has wisdom and a right to speak it. To make space for each person's whole being—body, mind, heart, and consciousness in every encounter. And I invite you to do the same for yourself as often as you can, including when you read this book.

Another take in this is that Pilates taught me to *allow, not force.* To create a container for sessions, classes, and experiences while modeling acceptance and integration. But within that, allow *their* timing, sensations, and body wisdom. There's truth and inspiration in letting people be themselves and learning the art of doing so yourself. There's also a gorgeous, unique rhythm, in it. We get to dance our dance and see that of others if we're successful at our love, creations, and teaching.

I can guide others to know their body, tendencies, tightnesses, and lead them to gently see what they may be holding. (It is possible to get more fluid at accepting oneself, surrendering what doesn't fit, and inviting what does to enter and take up space.)

It was and is through Pilates, imagery, creating trusting spaces, and modeling, that we all learned to stand taller in all of who we are. We all learned to listen and be more comfortable and coordinated in showing up as our full, integrated selves. I've taught and still teach repertoire and modifications but the I show you paradigm is outdated and unwelcome.

So imagine my surprise after 25 years of teaching in traditional gyms when I stepped off an elevator and into a simple, sunlight room with wood floors to learn Pilates. No music played and there were only two women waiting to answer my questions.

Was this business about to close? Where were the crowds? Where was the music? How do they get people to sign up? How do they get people to stay?

The desk by the door was small— like a child's desk. It was just big enough for a notepad, a bamboo plant, and a desktop computer. There were a few certificates on the wall, left of the door, and two pictures of Joe Pilates (*probably from the 1920's and*

1960's) on nearby walls. The walls were neutral colors and there were a few clipboards on the top counter.

I walked into a new way of being—a calmer, more connected way to live, move, and teach. It consisted of mutual conversation and deep engagement. During certification, and also in personal workouts, you were asked notice what bodies were saying in addition to how and what they said. Teaching was verbal and non-verbal, and it would be the template for every class, course, book, and offering I would ever create from that point. That paradigm shift translates to this book.

I no longer push and hustle. I offer. I demonstrate connection through offerings. This is one of them. Whether it's movement class or this book, I can help show you how to hear your breath and listen to your tissues, arms, heart, and belly. I can guide you to what's underneath. I can help you align your posture and elongate your spine so you have more space for life, confidence, and the vitality that is you.

Let's begin.

ONE
MODERN LIFE

The noise grew so loud she couldn't hear.
It was only then she realized she also couldn't see.

When you walk out of a movie theater and into a July afternoon in Texas, your eyes aren't the only things that need adjusting. Your body and senses scramble too. The contrast between a dark, loud, sixty-five degree theater and a sunny, Texas July day is a bit like a windowless basement in Boston in February and a frying pan.

Your eyes, skin, throat, even your hair have to adjust. Your sense of hearing, touch, and direction are disoriented. Your body and mind have been sitting in a movie theater absorbing a story at a hundred decibels for two and half hours. Your senses have adapted. Now you're asking them to return to the Texas sun, chirping birds, and your voice's natural volume.

After a few seconds, you find your feet. At that point, you can jump right back into to your chips and hot sauce, or you can pause and ask, "Are there any other situations in my life that may be like this?" "Are there additional times in my day when "noise" may be disorienting me?" "What might be the effect of this?"

To answer these, you need to know three things—*what noise is, where it might be in your life, and what disorientation feels like.* You have to pay attention. When you come out of a movie theater and onto a street at either noon or nine p.m., there are obvious contrasts. The street may be quieter or more stimulating than the theater. Most of us overlook the shift we need to make and just make it. Similar transitions are required when you go from an office building, a doctor's appointment, or an entertainment venue to your car. We get used to accommodating ourselves to the situation. Back and forth our body rhythms go without our attention. Before long, we adjust on autopilot all day long. We lose touch with ourselves, rationalize it, and block out the reality of how valuable we are.

But you have a natural rhythm within you—a speed, light, and environment in which you flourish best, have optimal clarity, wellbeing, and joy. It's a foundational premise of Ayurveda and Yoga,—the ancient holistic wisdom traditions of living in harmony with all that is. One of the most important things to know is this—**your body knows what your needs are.**

So what's noise to you? It depends on your natural state. And it can be hard to identify when we're not accustomed to listening. We dismiss *clatter, chatter, leaf blowers, dishwashers, alarms, dings, rings, blue light, a racing mind, car honks, fluorescent lights, radios, air pollution* and more in the name of getting along, going with the flow, normal expectations, getting a paycheck, and surviving.

But you deserve to bask in your timing, rhythm, and flow. You have the ability to experience your most balanced state, to touch divinity within you. It's your birthright to be in natural wellbeing, to feel your tissues hydrated in a way that makes you glide across the floor as you walk. It's not a dream. It's a possibility you can reproduce. Balance, equanimity, peace, and health are yours. They are for you.

If you study this book, allow yourself to read and sit with it, you can re-orient your senses and sense of self to a different kind of hearing and seeing. You can learn to spot noises more quickly and get more graceful at maintaining peace alongside them.

But one of the challenges is, it can be hard to hear noise when it's constant. Here's an invitation to turn it down. Adjust your eyes, ears, skin, arms, hair, and belly, and senses to a different view. A more peaceful view. One where you're at the center—aligned with beauty, harmony, and rhythm.

. . .

It's a skill you can carry everywhere, even into the movie theater.

- a prayer and a poem

The mind struggles with what the body knows.
The mind struggles with what the body feels.

The mind struggles today with what the body knew yesterday.

- heart breath

Oh, may I hear you! Oh, may I listen! Oh, may I bow to your
wisdom in my ears! May I love you as myself—

from within.
Your words pierce my ears heart, arms, and throat. From within,
you teach, hold, calm. From without, I reject, shush, and turn
away.

Forgive me, I am here, I am open, I am yours.
You are mine, me, now.

One breath and I am home.

- the heart pact

May I bend my knees, my will, my ways
and glide the rest of my hours
on your wings.

- splinters

Actions are like splintered wood, never knowing how far down
the beam they will carry.

It is often that an unsuspecting person picks up the wood,
quickly, *without pause*, hurrying along with her day—*little time
for interruption*—that she discovers her hand aches form the
intruder and her mind is full of the ache and her day is
suddenly nothing that she expected only an hour ago.

Books out, papers strewn, cold drinks, colored straws, and backpacks. A cornucopia of sights, sounds, energy piercing the air.

Sideways glances—

Who are you?

Who am I next to you?

- tick tock

Tick tock, tick tock

Your day was planned,
organized, sought.
All set out, but then—Surprise!
A move, a curve, a blow, a block.
Tick tock, tick tock.

An unexpected interruption
a cause-effect, a fierce assumption
about your day, about your say.
Tick tock, tick tock.

One little piece, one little play
one unplanned misstep on the way—
a morning bump that set you off
and now your time, *what was*, is lost.
Tick tock, tick tock.

Your day, now different

—it's trickled down
with bumps and bruises all along
and more and more, the bumps? They grow.
A tiny snowball from the snow.
Growing into something new
and making way for thoughts to brew.
Tick tock, tick tock.

Your day not yours.
Your soul not still.
You're caught up in the task, the drill.
You keep on running, down and low
but look at you—my precious soul!

See the wisdom, you can choose,
to live, to pause, to change the view.
Tick tock, tick tock.

The day that wasn't planned is now.
What will you choose? What will you do?
Shall you go on and run behind?
Or start afresh, anew this time?
Tick tock, tick tock.

- city sunrise

Orange sunrise, white moon at my back.
Trees, grasses, shrubs reach up
to majesty
as cars speed by, windows up.

.

- paper focus

Eyes on own paper.
But which paper?

- midday

Caffeine in hand—
warm and full,
I am again renewed.

The steam of which
drifts to my face
and vastly lifts my mood.

Thoughts are curious things. They seem to rise to the surface in a straight line as if they welled up from some clean, insulated pipe deep within us that is now delivering crisp, clear water. Someone might say, "I'm thinking about the kids," or "about a work task," or "going for a run" as if each of these arose on their own.

Thoughts don't spring from a single source. If they did—where is that exactly? When we grab one thought, it's more like a long-forgotten potato. By the time we find it, there are many eyes and it's hard to tell which one emerged first. And the bigger problem is, we think we have the potato when it's really just an eye.

- the whispers

Inside your heart
is a small chamber

of infinite possibilities,
authentic voice,
and blissful knowing.

This is where

The Whispers
l i v e.

And
b r e a t h e.

And
w a i t.

- love note

It's okay not to be okay.

Do not pretend to be strong for me—
I know you.

Cry, yearn, be sad, throw a fit. I have you.
Your tears, sorrow, and laughter are all the same to me—
all you.

Do not pretend to be unaffected by life, untouched by suffering.

Be in your humanity. Roll around in its bones. Become aware of
its sinews, shadows, and voids.

Swim in your waters, tendons, fat, muscle, connective tissue.
Feel your tautness, thickness, quality, and flow.

Hear your song, tempo, sound.

Live your beat and stillness. Lean into your resonance, rhythm, and sway. Tap flow and pause, tension and give, support and supported. Bones to bones and muscles to bones—all you.

Muscle, emotions, and thoughts run through. Feel the myriad. Feel the whole. Do not squash or squander your humanity. Love the light, caress the shadow, rock the welcome.

All you. All here. Now.

TWO
REALIZATION

She walked with hands outstretched as if driving an invisible car until her fingers wrapped around a metal gate leading to the sky.

And the gate led up to the sky. And the gate led up to the sky.

And the sky connected to earth.

And her fingertips wrapped around the essence of the divine right there on the metal. She stood in her own being and looked up, down, and felt in-between. She heard a knock in the distance and also within. Somewhere on the way to check the door and putting her hand on the handle, she found herself on a dark street. Black, still, quiet—except for a house at the end.

Her eyes narrowed to the porch light. It was small and in a metal holder that was slightly tilted, like it was hanging. There was a single flame inside, a dancing fire, and she became absorbed in it. Her whole body turned toward the light as if it could suck her up in a breath.

Forgetting her feet, her fingers still wrapped on the metal, she stood. She wasn't sure if she was blinking. For a moment, she wondered, *What did she look like standing there in front of the gate—stunned? Asleep? Would she hear if someone spoke to her?* But there she stood, focused on the light.

All noise disappeared, the day disappeared, and in a way, she disappeared. It was pleasant. All worries and rushing drained away, and only the center remained. It was utter freedom— just her, the dark, and the light.

-sky sublime

I went out for a drive and looked
at the sky and the road I took.
Speeding through, but slowing down
myself
I noticed the abundant view.

Why is it I can drive so far
and look around, and there you are?

Right, left, east, and west
around, above, behind, ahead?

Why is it that my world seems small
when I look up to you in awe?

You are vast and all around
you offer comfort, reality, ground.

Of who I am
and what is true—

I see the space between I and you
is vast a lie

and you are not

and what I need to do is stop

and rest in you—
the still, sublime

Connected deep in truth, in time.

- bluejay breakfast

There is a gem inside the shell.

Pick it up!

Examine it! Hug it! Thank it!

You are mine and
just for me.

All I had to do was

O
P
E
N

it.

- becoming art

Experiences make colorful indentations—bold chartreuse, velvety navy, or neon pink perhaps.

Some barely brush us, like water drops on a leaf after a spring rain. Others scratch, bruise, zigzag and traverse our life.

And some remove little pieces of us, like tiny rubber fragments torn from a small pink ball your dog played with.

Let the old pieces drift away—watch them float down a cool river where they will be cared for, but must go. See the tapestry that remains. Observe the colors and design. Feel the texture.

Drape it on your body and wear it with the skill with which it was woven.

- becoming

Becoming flows. Like water running through a house, it seeps into crevices, walls, and baseboards refusing containment. Faster and faster it weaves itself begging to express. It puddles in a corner here, covers new ground there. Soaks in, on, under.

When you try to wrap your arms around it, it slips through like a playful child.

Yes, no, maybe, I will, I won't, I see, I ignore. All habits, actions, thoughts, and emotions confirm this. The outer reflects the inner. The inner receives and recycles.

But if we are like Water, let us roll down the stairs with rhythm, flow, and force as the moment requires. Let us cool our feet, hands, and eyes with our dynamism. Let us bathe in *our* fragrance and nourish ourselves in the divinity of *our* moonlight.

If we are like River, let us stream across the earth, rocks, grasses, and a multitude of terrains with ease, mutability, and swiftness.

And if we are like Ocean, may we be full and fluid and bold in our girth. May we bask in *our* buoyancy, abundance, and depth.

May we feel *our* beat, bounce, crest! May we resist drought and breathe *our* reserves.

Oh, let us laugh as the ocean moves and move like the Ocean is!

Let us careen, drift, crash, and drip at times and places *we* need!

Above all, may we *choose* fluidity. May we intend the way for our being and being-ness. Turning up and tuning in, we roll.

Bringing, being, finding stillness as well as storm.

So that if we choose, we can stir our depths, unearth our core and soul and throw the pieces to the shores of life for all to see.

Allow the settled to become unsettled! Brave the removal! Refresh and turn the tide!

All this so we may encompass more, be more, become more. Be alive with your aliveness! Bring to the surface those settled pieces with gentle hands saying,

"Hey look at that! Now wash to the sand for those that may find you a treasure or carry yourself to the depths with the next wave!"

And when drought does arrive, as it sometimes tends to do, may you remember.

You are the Ocean.
You are the River.
You are the Source.

- becoming waves

Return to your tap and with a courageous and decisive will, turn the knob and rejoin the waves from which you came.

- choose

A stroke of genius,
A stroke of luck
It is my own
to tap

or buck.

- scavenger hunt

The seeds of a happy life are in the heart.
Crawled out and laid bare.

Waiting for you to

pick

them

up.

Life happens between spaces. We're always doing this then that, being this and that, going here then there, there then here. We achieve something we've never achieved, become someone we've never been. Who we are right now is in flow and created from an in-between.

Our hair, cells, bones and fascia communicate, grow, and release *in* the spaces. Who we were yesterday is never exactly who we are today. We are master mutators into the new, unpredictable, and unknown.

The fact that who we are changing into isn't clear or known until we arrive doesn't mean we aren't changing. Take it a step further and the space between the former and the new holds dozens, hundreds, tens of thousands of becoming moments. Who we are changing into remains mutable until we get there, yet never holds static upon arrival either, and this shows the vastness and quantity of the in-between.

Who we intend to become is one thing. Who we are on the journey can be a multitude of others. Who we become, yet another. There are resting spots, ledges, on which to breathe and celebrate the unknown. That's where becoming and unbecoming live.

That's where life is.

Whispering heart,
I see you there.
I hear your prompts,
I feel your stare.

Calling me, come home to you
where I can rest
and thrive
and bloom.

Snuggled up in you
I'm free
to laugh, to love, to experience me.

Shedding the mask, the shoulds, the hows,
the *I'm not good enough right now.*

And breathing in the truth of you,
of me,
of all there is to be.

All life ever was—was you
to have, to hold, to carry me through.

I hold in you the truth, the key
but it takes courage to set me free.

Wild and brazen grandiosity, of the quiet, the still, and simply

———

being.

- morning drive

I sit in the rush of traffic,
lanes full,
cars drive by.

Electric poles and ragged fences
line the path on our left side.

But off in the distance,
away from the road
sits a row of trees
with mist as clothes.

Taller ones
and younger too
up and down
around and through

the mist winds on,
their branches reach —
side to side
and below they meet

the grasses tall,
the birds above,
the sprawling sights
of nature's law.

Flowing one, still going on

no matter to what beat we drum.

Reminding us

of pause and breath,
speed and rest,
toil and best.

Within ourselves
we strum the chords, but within view?

There is more.

- lioness

I must come out,
I MUST! I say.

I see you there—
don't back away!

For I am here,
awaiting you,
holding space
for you—
YOUR truths.

Those knotty ones
that twist and dig
within your heart
and make you bleed?

Come claim your ground,
the space is yours—

to feel,
to fly,
to laugh
to roar!

There is enough to go around. The space right here—

your hallowed ground.

Make all the sound
you want, you need.

Speak!
Shout!

For now
you're
freed.

THREE
DEEPENING

Old trees have deep roots.

They've lived hard frosts, howling winds, snows, thaws, cold, dry, wet. They tap in and under knowing drought can come but connection is only a few feet away.

How many frosts have you lived? Winds, rains, and suns? How deep and vast are your roots?

Nourishment lives underground, a few feet from the surface. Living roots intertwine and support one another. They invest in, look out for, fight, commune, and communicate after sensing the needs of the other. They dance with the needs of other roots and share resources. They create and live in a vast landscape, a city-wide structure, and network.

Old roots—mangled, thick, and thin interweave like great arms from every culture and continent. They give stability and foundation. People walk freely near and around them, unaware and untroubled by the form, beauty, and cleansing they provide.

But there they are, like you, drinking in life, from base to limbs, growing beauty and reaching up to blue sky. You are a haven in which squirrels scamper, an owl burrows, and crows rest. You are home for many.

For now, you can rest too. For it is another season—a time to drop your leaves, surrender, and hold secure in the spring.

- Autumn, my muse.

Autumn is a muse I want to meet. I know she is there, right there around the corner, waiting for me, peeking at me from around the corner, she grins. She is like a child pretending to hide, but with her body visible from the edge. She stands at the corner as if peering around the edge of an old, two story, red brick building—the kind built thick and strong like they used to build. She is hiding and smiling, trying to wait, but knowing she cannot contain herself.

I see her—full of spirit, joy, and lightness—her energy bouncing toward me, inching to come near. Her colors cannot be withheld or delayed. Her vibrance cannot be hidden. She is waiting for Summer to finish her turn, to have her chance and time, to continue to heat up, burn and push and grind her way on passersby.

But her breezes seep out—red, orange, and gold leaves slip from her fingers and skip down the street, away from the edge of the building and into Summer's reach. Summer looks up—annoyed, scowling, heated, irritated, not ready to go, but knows she is no match. Knows she must go.

Autumn is too broad, too deep, too full of life and quiet strength. It is the smooth grace of Autumn that draws you in like music that soothes you to sleep before you realize you are drowsy.

Summer knows Autumn cannot be bound, cannot be boxed. She knows that when Autumn arrives, she must leave. But Summer holds on—glaring, gripping, defiant. Summer tries to buck up and pretend to be fierce and stalwart and firm, but she knows Autumn is too powerful, her beauty too alluring, her breezes too light and penetrating. She cannot prevent her reach, her breezes from spreading, soothing the cracks from Summer's scorn and seeping over and into the dry spaces. Autumn playfully suggests, hints, and whispers while growing stronger and cools the tired, worn earth beneath Summer's feet. Her nearness around the corner touches Summer's face.

Autumn fills the spaces between and around Summer's rough edges, her airiness sweeping the tiny cracks in the Earth.

Autumn whispers from the corner, "I am here," and Summer knows, she knows—she must go.

For Autumn cannot be contained, defined, or boxed by a "season". For she, Autumn, is *connection*, the bridge between the accusing, burning light of a sharp summer and the cruel unpredictability of a frozen winter. For she, Autumn, is soft and fluid. She is the melody that enchants, a lullaby for trees, the air in between.

The middle way wins.

- old trees

Old trees- sticks, and brooms and raw thunderbolts ready for massive rudders and kitchen tables. The tips of its branches appearing to hang on by a thread—broken, torn, willingly dropping into a graveyard of sticks below. Standing strong in its history and tradition, knowing what's true, what is, what it needs, and where it belongs.

A support structure reaching across the lawn and towards the street—a table underneath a cloth.

A hidden bridge for cars and pedestrians unaware they are walking on an ancient system of communication, an ecosystem, a trade system, a protection system. Intertwining and sending messages, nutrients, and rest below and above.

Making a home and offering in the dark as well as light.

Drinking in the new, pulling it up through its core— a straw of the now, in the middle of what was. A force upon the earth, digging down, yet gazing up.

Their steadiness is my reserve. Their community, my heart. Their reach, my goal.

- country road

Mid-day pick me up
I forgot to tell it where

and so it drove and drove
through fields of country air
I smelled the grass, felt the breeze, fingers open wide
drawing in majestic earth
into my lungs,
and hands,
and eyes.

Hair afloat with crazed excitement, flapping in the wind.
Face absorbing light and warmth, exposing gentle grin.

Elbow leaning farther now—out against the wind
from the car as I went traveling
from my kitchen coffee tin.

- cream cheese at night

The moon soothes me,
like cream cheese on bread.
Spread on an even, thick layer
using a cool utensil and a smooth stroke.

Cool refreshment
when I am dry, stuck, burnt, crumpled up
like dry toast,
with crispy edges flaking off in the palm of my hand.

Cool nourishment
holding me
as my thumbs hold
the burnt corners.

Cool moisture—
you glue everything together
and make everything
more palatable.

All my worries, fears, irritations
smoothed out. The world goes down more easily now,

in
one
big
bite.

-my backyard at night

A tree, string lights
some jazz (*manouche*),
white moonlight.

Trickling down in powdery flakes
melting it's glow
onto my arms, head, neck, face.

Cooling now,
soaking it in
spreading peace, equanimity
across my spine, back, toes, shins.

Whole body beaming
receiving your light
I come home to you--
I am filled with your sight.

Playful, alive,
like a child, I dance
I twirl unafraid
and I bask and I laugh.

Then I lie outstretched
with hands on the grass
Earth as my bed
and you, moon, overhead

directing a choir, a symphony, a song
of all us together,
right here—
we belong.

The stars play a tune
you, moon, at the helm

we each play a part of a journey, an art.

Filling our hearts,
hands, homes, and being
our speech and our voice,
our arms and our land.

We learn and we grow.
We reach, we receive.
We mirror the light —

reflect you,
see me.

My oasis is yours
and yours becomes me.

With feet in the grass
we are all of one sea.

- surrender

Surrender the struggle,
the tousle,
the fight

of me over you,
wrong versus right

Open hands, flowing free
relinquish the war

and let it be.

- magnolia tree

Today I looked at a magnolia tree in my yard. By all accounts it's an ugly, disorderly tree. It's been there twelve years.

Someone planted it a foot from the side of a two-story house. So a wall of red bricks forms the backdrop, like a billboard with a tree graphic printed on one side.

It has only about three feet of soil from front to back and maybe ten feet from side to side. It has another few feet to grow in the front once it gets out of the soil. Side to side, it has more than enough space to grow, but the back is stunted due to the wall.

It's been there twelve years, so it's adapted. It grows a little here and there with twigs sprouting off a thin, wavy trunk that looks like an arm holding a bouquet of flowers, but most of the flowers have blown away now.

In front of the tree, there's a roof that partially blocks the sun, and so I suppose that's part of the reason the trunk is wavy —in search of sunlight. The back side looks flattened, adolescent. The other—bouncy, full, vibrant.

I look at the wiry little branches hanging low, tiny twigs at random spots and places— two on the left, three on the right. They look like mistakes so I pull them off.

I love this tree. It reminds me of me. Of us. Of mistakes and imperfections we want to pull off too. We don't want to see them and we don't want others to either. Sometimes we lack growing space and we change directions and plans—moving around, up, and out in order to get the sun we need.

And yet, the skinny tree persists. It reaches upward and out where it can and uses its base to grow more leaves so it can have more nutrients. It persists, overcomes, thrives. It may not reach its full potential on one side, but it's certainly tying to make up for it on the other.

It can bloom and so it does. White, fragrant petals open just as large as on a big magnolia tree on a Southern lawn. It doesn't feel less or wonder if it can bloom because it's small, looks disorderly, or feels cramped. It just blooms.

It basks in the sun, but also knows how to grow in the dark. It's now tall enough to bypass the roof, and continues unstoppable seeking sun where it can.

- stethoscope

Listen to your heart.
Listen to your heart whispers.
Listen to your heart whispers, they know.
Listen to your heart whispers, they know how.
Listen to your heart whispers, they know how to love you.

Listen to your heart whispers, they know how to love you best.

- the dinner party, 1

One step at a time,
they all come in
visitors teaching me love, compassion,
starting again.

Clearing the way for something new
shedding the old, welcoming truth.

Opening the doors to who I am
learning my stride from fall to grin.

With every step I'm more myself
I drink in love, I walk in health.

Connected now in every way
I sit with them—I feast, I play.

All the different sides of me,
here at night and also day

no more hiding them —
the loud,
the *yes I've got this*,
I'll take my bow.

They are free and fun and here
exactly how they are—appeared.

They have flow and bounce and rest
precisely when it serves *them* best.

Spread out now
with food and drink
they eat, they talk,
and build their strength.

Unafraid to taste at will
they flavor sounds, house, and sill.

They drink and laugh
and pass the flask.
They toast and cheer
and raise a glass
to me—

for showing up tonight,

letting them in,
and taking flight.

- thawed out

The covered sun,
the barren tree,
the frost of winter
holding me

But it is spring, I must come out!

From underneath my fear, my doubt.

Hello! I've missed you!
Come on in—

The breath, the voice

of me—

I Am.

- hue

In and out
and left and right,
I look, I hope...

for clarity, for sight.

To see what is,
what was, is true
behind the mask of modern hue.

I long to sit and be with you,
to rest in space,
to breathe your moods.

To see, say, taste your name
to hear your sound
to dance your ways.

Infuse me with your grace at last!
That I may toast and raise a glass
to touching deep, *to brewing you*
in all I think, and say, and do.

Within my soul, my heart, my mind
unleash the clear,
unwrap divine!

Wash my eyes, my ears, my face
surround me in perfumed embrace.

That I may cast a golden hue
in all I walk, and say, and do.

A spark, a light, a golden rim
painting all
with bliss and grin.

My heart is full, it leaps for joy
that you are near, but far away
I look for you without, not in.
I plead, I ask to come, befriend

my heart, my hands ,my mouth, my feet
that I may do, tell, say, teach

Your words so clear I'll know at once
it's you who talks—it's you who speaks.

What's that you say?
Search not my friend
just stop and breathe—
enter in.

You're touching grace right here, right now.
You're the vessel, you're the plow.

Sowing seeds
and reaping grains
absorbing light
and spreading rains

with all you speak and say and do
you deliver me—
my grace,
my truth.

- lover's kiss

For I have met you once before
your love, compassion
your welcome—
warm.

Inviting me to come and sit
to stay,
to breath,
to drink you in.

Ego gone,
arms spread wide,
I inhale joy,
I unclasp pride.

Heart flowing,
embracing all,
your wings gliding me to All.

Beneath my arms,
the air I breathe—
your taste remains—
abundant sea.

Untainted bliss
And here we sit,
you and I—

a lover's kiss.

FOUR
HOME

And for a moment the world was still.

She glided in her own energy, heard birdsong, and felt in tune
with the seasons, trees, and even leaves. Like them, she
made her own music as she moved.

She was within and without.

Time passes quickly when you're enveloped. When you're in a flow greater than ordinary life. And what's ordinary about it? What's "regular" about being alive? What's "normal" about blood flowing through your veins, plasma and lymph working all day long for your wellbeing? To have a network of fascia—lateral, vertical, diagonal, and spiral to hold you up? Wells for your bones? Legs in sockets, and a spirit that begs to soar and sing your truth from five a.m.?

Tasks, calendars, worries, to-do's may insinuate both you and your life are ordinary. They may demand their importance, immediacy, and how *they* define *you*. But when you realize you're connected to seasons, the moon, ocean tides, and birdsong, something remarkable happens—you see outside of yourself. You grow. The expression of who you are emerges. You become on the outside who you are on the inside.

Your eyes, ears, lips, and skin taste truth—you are magnificent. You are divine. You are as expansive as the Earth and deep as the ocean.

This book is an attempt to awaken those truths and invite you to remember them.

- what senses are for

Nose in a cup
spicy fog to my lips.
Eyes, nose, ears, mouth,
ingest warmth, surrender—
what is.

Smelling, seeing flowers
breathing stillness, beauty, being.

A bath of sweet aromas,
A song of lavender I sing.

I wrap myself in softness,
caress my silky skin

and now I sit surrounded
by a symphony of Zen.

With hands in the dirt
and on bended knees,
I come to you
to set me free.

Release my sorrows!
Free my grief!

Rise exuberance! Joy!

Defeat

is no more
because

I am you.

Your truth, beauty now flow through.

- tango

A dance of seasons,
times,
places.

A dance of wind,
sun,
moon,
spaces.

Flowing,
now still,
then firing up!

I am one with nature,

I drink her cup.

- take a drink

Giving up
and giving in
surrender to the sound—

within

the breath, the arms, the back, the throat
it carries me like clouds, remote.

Far away I go, right here
I sit and breathe—stars, moon, seers

For what is time?
How long it's been
spinning souls and morphing plans.

And vast between your world and mine
is you and I—

we drink divine

Inside my chest, inside my being

I feel your light,
I hear your ring.

Into my ears of what is true—

I sit with you

and you

and you.

- prayer of moonbeams

Dear heart,

Flow through my being with your magnetic attraction. Fill my blood, cells, face, and organs with your unwavering force, your courage, and your right now, bold, embracing love! Drip your sweet nectar onto and into my life. Fill my eyes with compassion and the ability to see as you do. Light my interior like moonbeams until my fingers, toes, and tongue drip golden.

- the messenger

Open the channel,
Allow it to flow
You are the conduit.

The messenger

The message.

Dark blue sky—cold and smooth
A placid lake of inner truth.

And deep within?
A moon aglow.
Stark white moonbeams —ice and snow.

Icy sheen of solid white
strong, complete, radiant light.

With snowy rim—a powdery dew
to soften the edges and carry the hue.

Throughout the sky, which mirrors me—
gentle white snowflakes throughout my being.

The moon, my soul, with piercing light
stabbing the darkness, giving me sight.

The powdery snowflakes drift around
and float throughout
my body,
my mind,
my bounds.

Connected here my soul can roam
At last, I'm free—

I'm here.
I'm home.

- the vessel

Open the flow and there you are,
Holding the divine within you.

Expansive,
Bright,
Knowing,
Focused,
Calm,
Piercing,

Blissful.

Belonging to you, belonging to me
I see the connection
from my head to your feet.

Thriving together
not two, but one
our souls on a journey
to learn, grow, become.

The light we project,
we bathe in, we send.

It travels from core
and then whirls back in.

Through the other, from all around
we exist in vibration,
energy,
sound

to our ears
our heart
our mind--
it ignites!

It glows
and it speaks.
It calms and delights!

It's all that is,
does,
and can be--

that light within you,
is the light within me.

- interior song

See with your eternal eyes

hear with your eternal ears

taste with your eternal mouth

and
when
you
speak

you will hear your eternal song.

- the walk

I went outside and there you were, wildly extending an invitation to be with you, walk with you, confess to you.

I felt your presence, warmth, and love and so I could not resist. We walked together in the morning light—cool and rising. You knew my sorrow, grief, and longing. You welcomed me as I am. You invited me to be myself.

You reminded me I am more than body and task. I am creative energy full of life. You showed me who I am meant to be. I felt free, unencumbered. My mind and body were opened, my spirit soared. My heart lifted.

You motioned me to sit with you and I could not resist your beauty, call, embrace, and abundance.

Your essence moved me. I felt your nature and I could not resist your invitation to be myself. And so I did.

We had warm sun shining through the tops of the pines as we walked. We had moments of quiet, and I could hear the crunch of leaves and gravel under my shoes. I heard a bird call to others, singing, as if to say,

"She is here! She is home!"

You encouraged me to share my story, release my sadness, and open my heart. I poured myself out to you, on to you, and you did not retract, wince, or fade. You stood strong but soft, able to hear my truth and offer a new becoming, a new perspective through your presence.

I felt loved, cared for, renewed. We sat right there in the forest, back to back. The sun warmed our ears, shoulders, back, and arms. I was different than only an hour ago. Calmer. Sadness and longing had leaked out. In its place, there was an opening for something I hardly recognized.

I felt a light fleck of gold in the middle of my chest. I only caught a glimpse, but could feel its power.

"That's you," I heard the tree whisper.

"Why have I never known it? Where has it come from?" I asked.

"That's your spirit, your knowing. It's been you all along. All you had to do was remove the veil so you could see it."

Renewed,
I thanked the tree.
I thanked the forest for its welcome,
the bird for its song.

I am here.
I am home.

EXTRA CHAPTERS ARE LIKE SPICE
WHAT'S COOKING?

Chapters after a book's natural ending are like spices—salt, mustard, ginger, cinnamon, pepper. How do they flavor the book? Does it become more edible? Desirable? Sour? Does the story meal go down easier? Digest more fully? Does it make you crave it more? This reminds me of Stephen King.

In 1999, Stephen King was writing *On Writing*—a book I recommend for all creatives and most people. There are no gruesome stories in it except for this one. In the postscript, he tells us that he wrote part of the book while recuperating from a vehicular collision. He was on foot. A van hit him from the highway. While writing the book, he had eight screw-type devices bolted into his leg. These were routinely removed, cleaned by alcohol, and reinserted. He endured five surgeries to be able to walk again. He gives details about the incident and his recuperation which I won't include any more here, but you get the picture. Makes me appreciate the story more.

The reason for this particular "extra" is to tell you this: You can't max out on the good stuff. You can't overload, overeat, or overstuff yourself on truth, beauty, self-love, self-compassion, kindness, or centeredness. Can you be too happy? Too well? Too loving? Too aligned?

There's no barrier to anything you want in life, and there's (*likely*) no barrier to getting it. If one exists, it's so far away, you're much more likely to grow, receive, and experience goodness without ever encountering it.

Owning our agency—our voice, decisions, actions, reactions, past, present, and future, is one of the most constructive and difficult things we can do. I've found it to be a great secret locked in a small box—like a condiment drawer or spice rack that's abundant, but rarely used.

Every time you hear, "I can't," "You can't," "Who do you think you are,?" or "Look at me, I'm better than you," return to this or another book that helps you connect to and enliven your Spirit. Its flavors help you absorb the food of life.

It can be hard to give ourselves the medicine we need, the suggested spices for optimal wellbeing. We may fear the taste, effects, or our identity as a person who cooks or eats in a certain way.

Perhaps it's ridiculous to imagine we'd reject something "good" for us, like cumin in rice or cardamom in tea, but the subconscious mind runs somewhere between **88-97%** of daily operations and if you've got a positive association with ice cold water and a meal, you're probably going to keep doing it unless or until you understand it extinguishes your metabolic fire and you decide you'd rather feel better. I don't care if you have cold water with your meals. You can have the cold water or not. I'm just saying that some habits (*and chapters*) affect the whole meal.

Believing you can do more, be more, and have more joy and wellbeing every day is like coming home to soup on the stove with balanced spices. The aroma fills your home, throat, mind, and belly.

For now, let it be spring for your heart, mind, and spirit.

Wellbeing is yours. It's time to flower. If you turn the pages of this book with love and a sincere desire for growth, the gardens of your heart and life will bloom.

May we all have the proper type and amount of spice in our life to open our heart, eyes, and belly to truth.

A WORD

DOES IT WORK?

This book isn't going to solve all your problems. Not even one. It's only a book. And anyway, only you can do that. But if you read it, study it, and allow it into your heart, it can be a guide for *you changing you*. Think of it as a wedding invitation lingering on your counter, a message on your phone, a note on your desk—"Read me. Become me. Know who you are".

What's a problem, anyway? Every stress, worry, doubt, and anxiety is an opportunity. Every nagging, uncomfortable, or frustrating situation is just that— a situation. You can view them as downers, pesky trash in the way of your otherwise beautiful walk. You can see challenges as keeping you from the money, relationships, health, or life you want. But you can also use them as fuel and lessons. You can look to them as guide-posts to steer your journey.

Your challenges, (*and everyone has some*), don't glue your bum to the seat of your current life or keep you on a hamster wheel that prevents your dreams. I learned from a mentor, problems are a good thing. You have the option to think of them as negative, (*and yourself as negative too*), but that's a wheel that can go on forever.

The way out, the way to *freedom* is **dancing your dance.** That means accepting all of who you are as often as you can. Now. Accepting what *is* and *accepting you.* Do it again. Do it again. Do it as many times as it takes to actually accept your preferences, voice, history, and body. Why? Acceptance says yes to what is and that's saying yes to life. When you do that, Spirit can show you more.

Greater autonomy, clarity, vibrance, and utter wellbeing flow in like breezes right outside your door. And by the way, you get to name who or what Spirit is for you. But connect to that force, energy, utter goodness. Tap the Source of all creativity, being, and life. That's what this book is about.

I'm not trying to make it sound easy. It depends. It's easy to know you're Spirit—it only takes a second, maybe less. The veil is thin from here to there. But it's difficult to take the leap and *keep* taking it because comparison and self-defeating messages are everywhere. We have a lifetime, (*or several depending on your beliefs*), of inculturation from families, society, neighborhoods, religion, schools, and media that constantly suggest we may not be enough. That we're lacking.

How do you break through? How can this book guide you to more peace alongside daily messages to the contrary and a history of unhelpful programming? It's work you do by allowing. By reading, re-reading, and breathing in words that help you see you. Open the door to deeper healing, a clearer vision, attuned hearing. Allow the words to hydrate your fascia, tissues, and heart. Surrender your senses and listen.

Here's my invitation. Choose you. Listen to your heart and allow yourself to *re-tune* to magnificence.

I walk with you.

INDEX

FIND YOUR POEM

What inspires you? Nature? People? The divine? Whichever it is (*or multiple*), you can find them here with ease. And, you can spot patterns and changes here too.

Poems are organized by obvious theme. (*A poem about sky is in nature section.*) However, as you know, a poem can fit multiple categories. In that case, you'll find it under several headings.

For electronic versions, poems are listed by the chapter number followed by where it's placed in the chapter. For example, the second poem in chapter two, *Realization*, is noted as 2.2. The third poem in chapter two is 2.3. For print versions, page numbers are given as expected.

Happy reading!

Calm

Autumn, My Muse, 40-41
Becoming, 26-27
Becoming Art, 24-25
Cream Cheese at Night, 44
Heart Breath, 6
Hue, 54-55
Love Note, 17-18
My Backyard at Night, 45-46
On Meditation, 66-67
Prayer of Moonbeams, 64
The Whispers, 16
What Senses are for, 59
Whispering Heart, 32-33

Divine

Belonging to You, 69-70
Hue, 54-55
Interior Song, 71
Lover's Kiss, 56
My Backyard at Night, 45-46
On Meditation, 66-67
Prayer of Moonbeams, 64
Sky Sublime, 21-22
Take a Drink, 62-63
The Gardener's Prayer, 60
The Messenger, 65
The Vessel, 68
The Walk, 72-73

Integration / Becoming

A Prayer and a Poem, 5
Autumn, My Muse, 40-41
Becoming, 26-27
Becoming Art, 24-25
Becoming Waves, 28
Bluejay Breakfast, 23
Cream Cheese at Night, 44
Heart Breath, 6
Hue, 54-55
Lioness, 36-37
Love Note, 17-18
Lover's Kiss, 56
Magnolia Tree, 48-49
My Backyard at Night, 45-46
Old Trees, 42
Scavenger Hunt, 30
Sky Sublime, 21-22
Spaces, 31
Take a Drink, 62-63
Tango, 61
Thawed Out, 53
The Dinner Party I, 51-52
The Gardener's Prayer, 60
The Heart Pact, 7
The Thinking Pipeline, 15
The Walk, 72-72
The Whispers, 16
Whispering Heart, 32-33

Nature & Animals

Autumn, My Muse, 40-41
Becoming, 26-27
Becoming Waves, 28
Bluejay Breakfast, 23
City Sunrise, 12
Country Road, 43
Lioness, 36-37
Magnolia Tree, 48-49
Morning Drive, 34-35
My Backyard at Night, 45-46
Old Trees, 42
On Meditation, 66-67
Sky Sublime, 21-22
Tango, 61
The Gardener's Prayer, 60
The Walk, 72-73

People

A Prayer and a Poem, 5
Becoming, 2.4
Becoming Art, 24-25
Becoming Waves, 28
Bluejay Breakfast, 23
Choose, 29
City Sunrise, 12
Cream Cheese at Night, 44
4:48, 9
Heart Breath, 6
Lionness, 36-37
Love Note, 17-18
Midday, 14

Magnolia Tree, 48-49

Paper Focus, 13

Splinters, 8

Stethoscope, 50

Surrender, 47

Thawed Out, 53

The Dinner Party, 1, 51-52

The Heart Pact, 7

The Thinking Pipeline, 15

Tick Tock, 10-11

Whispering Heart, 32-33

Places

Country Road, 43

4:48, 9

Morning Drive, 34-35

My Backyard at Night, 45-46

The Walk, 72-73

ABOUT THE AUTHOR

Melissa Monroe is a lifelong poet, nonfiction, and fiction writer. She's also the founder of Rooted Wholeness, a wellness center where she teaches Pilates, Ayurveda, and Energy work, and has an Ayurvedic farm in the making.

She believes we are one humanity, and love really is the way. You can often find her near sparkly lights, on walks, sipping tea, and communing with nature and the subtle energies of everyday life.

Zen in the City is her debut poetry collection and this is the debut book for Rooted Wholeness Press.

Writing @Melissa-monroe.com and @melissa_monroewriter

Rooted Wholeness @rootedwholeness.com